CODE READER™

Making Difficult Words Easy

Code Reader Books provide codes with "sound keys" to help read difficult words. For example, a word that may be difficult to read is "unicorn," so it might be followed by a code like this: unicorn *(YOO-nih-korn)*. By providing codes with phonetic sound keys, Code Reader Books make reading easier and more enjoyable.

Examples of Code Reader™ Keys

Long a sound (as in make):
a *(with a silent e)* or **ay**
Examples: able *(AY-bul)*; break *(brake)*

Short i sound (as in sit): **i** or **ih**
Examples: myth *(mith)*; mission *(MIH-shun)*

Long i sound (as in by):
i *(with a silent e)* or **y**
Examples: might *(mite)*; bicycle *(BY-sih-kul)*

Keys for the long o sound (as in hope):
o *(with a silent e)* or **oh**
Examples: molten *(MOLE-ten)*; ocean *(OH-shen)*

Codes use dashes between syllables *(SIH-luh-buls)*, and stressed syllables have capital letters.

To see more Code Reader sound keys, see page 44.

GORILLA

VERSUS LION

HEAD-TO-HEAD

Written by
Noah Leatherland

TREASURE BAY

Gorilla versus Lion: Head-to-Head

A Code Reader™ Chapter Book
Green Series

This book was created by BookLife Publishing under agreement with Treasure Bay, Inc. Copyright © 2025 Treasure Bay, Inc.

Code Reader™ is a trademark of Treasure Bay, Inc.

Reading Consultant: Jennifer L. VanSlander, Ph.D., Asst. Professor of Educational Leadership, Columbus State University

Patent Pending.
Code Reader books are designed using an innovative system of methods to create and include phonetic codes to enhance the readability of text.
Reserved rights include any patent rights.

All images are courtesy of Shutterstock.com.
Recurring – Tabata Art Studio. Cover – OSDG, Eric Isselee. 2–3 – Petr Muckstein, Wirestock Creators, Eric Isselee. 4–5 – Lance van de Vyver, asim younus. 6–7 – LouieLea, Howard Darby, Eric Isselee, dhtgip. 8–9 – Adrian Dockerty, Eric Isselee, Mary Ann McDonald, Mike Price. 10–11 – Sharon Shaw, Eric Isselee, sasha_gerasimov. 12–13 – N. F. Photography, asim younus, Clive Anders, TravellingFatman. 14–15 – Eric Isselee, Smileus. 16–17 – MintImages, Kirill Dorofeev, Francois van Heerden. 18–19 – J_K, Elagina, CreativeWILD - CS. 20–21 – Tadan, Erni, LuismiCSS. 22–23 – Pakalou, Alan Tunnicliffe, Steven Litton. 24–25 – Photos of Africa, Alta Oosthuizen, Wirestock Creators, Maggy Meyer. 26–27 – Dane Jorgensen, Alexandra Giese, photomaster. 28–29 – Eric Isselee, Sergey Uryadnikov. 30–31 – Volodymyr Burdiak, Sykes Images. 32–33 – Seyms Brugger, marian78ro, Funny Solution Studio, weicool. 34–35 – PHOTOCREO Michal Bednarek, emin kuliyev, photomaster. 36–37 – SteffenTravel, enciktat, Tanya Puntti. 38–39 – e2dan, Dan OFlynn. 40–41 – Philippe Clement, Hurst Photo, RIck Massar Photography, Juliya_be_cool.

Published by Treasure Bay, Inc.
PO Box 519, Roseville, CA 95661 USA

Printed in China

Library of Congress Control Number: 2024944969

ISBN: 978-1-60115-723-2

Visit us online at: CodeReader.org

PR-1-25

CONTENTS

Words that look like **this** are explained in the glossary or in an orange *(OR-unj)* box like this one.

ANIMAL VERSUS ANIMAL

The animal kingdom is full of deadly fighters *(FY-turz)*. For lots of animals, being good at fighting is an important part of survival *(sur-VY-vul)*. They might need to fight for food, for their homes, or to protect themselves. Sometimes, they need to fight for their lives!

There are so many skilled fighters in the animal kingdom . . . but which one is the best? Which animal could take on all the others and come out on top?

2

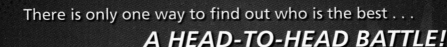

There is only one way to find out who is the best . . .

A HEAD-TO-HEAD BATTLE!

In the blue corner, the prowling predator of the **savannah** (suh-VAN-uh) . . . **THE AFRICAN** (AF-rih-kin) **LION!**

In the red corner, the **toughest** (TUF-ist) **primate** (PRY-mate) in the jungle . . . **THE SILVERBACK GORILLA!**

Toughest
strong and hard to break (brake)

It is time to find out which **competitor** (kum-PEH-tih-tur) is the best fighter. Let's take a look at these brutal (BROO-tul) beasts and see how they compare.

THE AFRICAN LION

Male lions fight to protect the group *(groop)* from other animals. Female *(FEE-male)* lions fight to hunt for food.

Weight: Around 500 pounds

Length: Around 10 feet from nose to tip of the tail

Top Speed: 50 miles per hour

Aggression *(uh-GREH-shun)*: High

Diet *(DY-et)*: Meat

Found in: Africa *(AF-rih-kuh)*

Habitat: Savannah and grasslands

Best weapons *(WEH-punz)*: Teeth and claws

Aggression
how violent *(VY-oh-lint)* or prepared to attack

THE SILVERBACK GORILLA

There are two main **species** (*SPEE-sheez*) of gorilla. They are the western gorilla and the eastern gorilla.

Species
the different types of animals

Weight: Around 500 pounds

Length: Around 6 feet tall when standing

Top Speed: 25 miles per hour

Aggression: High, but only when angry

Diet: Plants, fruit, and insects

Found in: Africa

Habitat: Jungles and forests

Best weapons: Fangs, hands, and strength

FIGHTER PROFILES

THE KING OF BEASTS

The African lion is one of the most well-known big cats in the world. Big cats have a lot of things in **common** (KAH-mun) with the cats that people (PEE-pul) keep as pets. They have whiskers, paws, and tails that all look similar to what smaller cats have.

However, big cats such as lions are much larger and are much deadlier (DED-lee-ur) beasts. Big cats have large paws, long claws, and huge (hyooj) teeth.

Lions live in groups called prides. Prides can have just a few *(fyoo)* lions in them, or they can have as many as 40 lions. African lions are found in parts of sub-Saharan *(sub-suh-HARE-un)* Africa. They live on grassy plains called savannahs *(suh-VAN-uz)*.

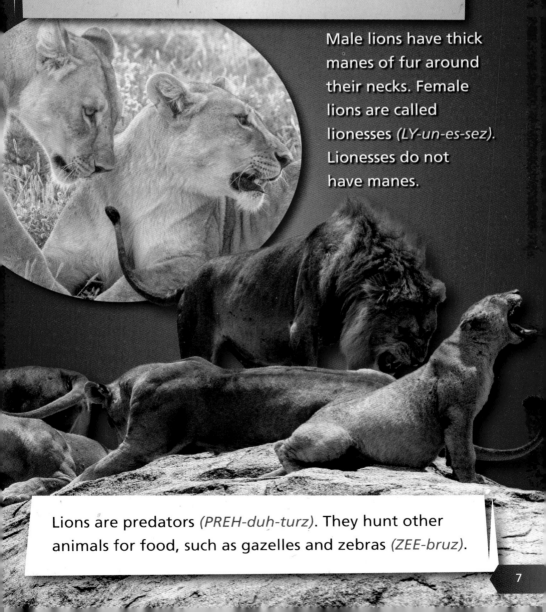

Male lions have thick manes of fur around their necks. Female lions are called lionesses *(LY-un-es-sez)*. Lionesses do not have manes.

Lions are predators *(PREH-duh-turz)*. They hunt other animals for food, such as gazelles and zebras *(ZEE-bruz)*.

Gorillas are the largest primates on the planet. Primates are a group of animals that include *(in-KLOOD)* monkeys, chimpanzees, and even humans *(HYOO-munz)*.

Silverback gorillas are not a separate *(SEH-pur-et)* species of gorilla. Instead, silverback gorillas are fully grown male gorillas. They are called silverbacks because of the color of their fur. As young male gorillas get older, the fur on their back turns a silvery gray color. Silverbacks are the most powerful members of a group.

Gorillas live in groups in the forests and jungles of central *(SEN-trul)* Africa. Groups of gorillas are called troops. Troops can have just a few gorillas in them, or up to 50 gorillas.

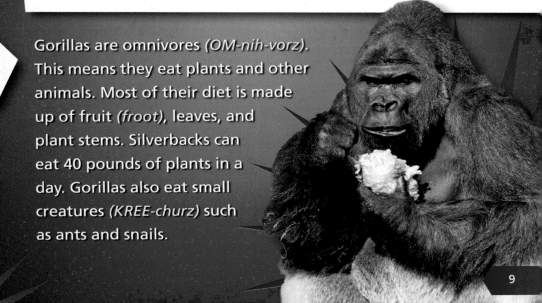

Gorillas are omnivores *(OM-nih-vorz)*. This means they eat plants and other animals. Most of their diet is made up of fruit *(froot)*, leaves, and plant stems. Silverbacks can eat 40 pounds of plants in a day. Gorillas also eat small creatures *(KREE-churz)* such as ants and snails.

ANIMAL WEAPONRY
(WEH-pun-ree)
FROM TOOTH TO PAW

Lions have very deadly teeth. Their teeth help them tear *(tair)* meat apart when they eat. They are also useful *(YOOS-ful)* weapons for fighting and hunting!

Lions have four large canine *(KAY-nine)* teeth. These canine teeth can grow to around three inches long. They are perfect for biting into **prey** *(pray)*. A lion's jaws are so powerful that just one bite can kill an animal.

Prey
animals that are hunted by other animals for food

Lions have large paws. The deadliest parts of their paws are their sharp claws. These claws can grow up to one and a half (haf) inches long.

Lions mainly use their claws to grip. Their claws are very helpful for climbing (KLY-ming). However, the most important thing that lions need to grip onto is their prey. Lions dig their claws into their prey and hold on tight before delivering a killer bite.

GORILLA:
TOOTH TO PALM (pom)

Although *(awl-THO)* gorillas do not do much hunting, they have some pretty sharp fangs in their mouths. These fangs can grow up to two inches long.

Gorillas use their pointy fangs to **intimidate** *(in-TIM-ih-date)* others. They show off their fangs to try to stop a fight from happening. But these fangs are not just for show. Gorillas are not afraid *(uh-FRADE)* to use them in a fight and cut into an enemy.

Intimidate
to frighten someone
into doing something

You can see how closely gorillas are related to humans by looking at their hands. Gorillas have fingers and thumbs (*thumz*), just like humans do. Thumbs are extremely (*ex-TREEM-lee*) helpful for grabbing things.

Gorillas use their hands for lots of things, from grooming each other to picking up food. Gorillas have been seen picking up rocks and sticks to use as tools. Being able (*AY-bul*) to grab things easily (*EEZ-zih-lee*) could be very helpful in a fight against (*uh-GENST*) a lion. . . .

STRENGTH AND POWER

Lions have a lot of **muscle** *(MUS-sul)* under their fur. Their muscles are perfect for short bursts of energy, such as leaping and sprinting.

Muscle
body parts that move the body around

Lions are around seven times stronger than a human. They can jump more than three times as far as a human being can. Lions can bite with the **force** of around 1,000 pounds per square inch. That is enough *(ee-NUF)* force to snap bones!

Silverback gorillas are said to be able to lift around ten times their body weight *(wate)*. Some say silverbacks are over eight times stronger than a human. Imagine *(im-MAJ-in)* what that sort of power could do in a fight!

Gorillas also have an incredibly strong bite force. They can bite with 1,300 pounds per square inch of force—even *(EE-ven)* more bite force than a lion!

Gorillas have been seen tearing entire trees apart to eat what is inside.

ANIMALS IN ACTION

It is the male lions' job to protect the group. Although lions are the top predators of their habitats, other animals still try to pick a fight. Sometimes, a lion might have to fight off other groups of lions.

Male lions mark the **territory** *(TAIR-ih-TOR-ee)* of their pride. Lions spread their **urine** *(YUR-in)* so that other animals can smell that they are nearby.

Territory
an area of land that something rules over

Urine
the proper word for pee

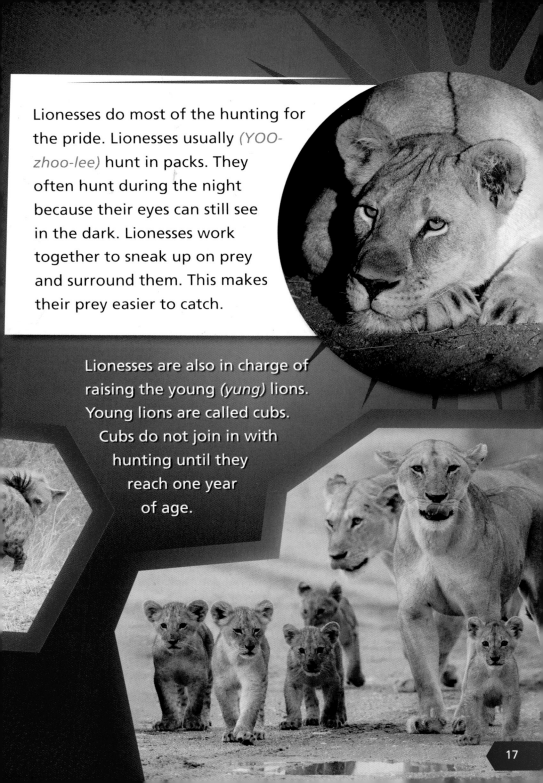

Lionesses do most of the hunting for the pride. Lionesses usually *(YOO-zhoo-lee)* hunt in packs. They often hunt during the night because their eyes can still see in the dark. Lionesses work together to sneak up on prey and surround them. This makes their prey easier to catch.

Lionesses are also in charge of raising the young *(yung)* lions. Young lions are called cubs. Cubs do not join in with hunting until they reach one year of age.

Male lions have to be careful of other male lions. Usually, a pride has one **dominant** *(DAH-mih-nent)* male in charge. There may be other males in the pride as well. If there are, the males may fight over who is in charge.

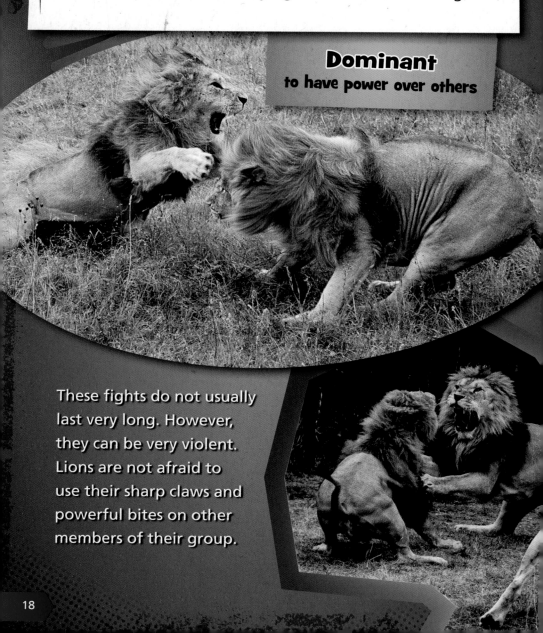

Dominant
to have power over others

These fights do not usually last very long. However, they can be very violent. Lions are not afraid to use their sharp claws and powerful bites on other members of their group.

Lions have to keep an eye on male lions that are outside, as well as inside, of their group. Male cubs are often kicked out of their pride when they are a few years old.

A few of these young males sometimes form a small group called a **coalition** *(ko-uh-LISH-un)*. These coalitions look for other prides. Coalitions attack the dominant males to take over as the new leaders of the group.

Coalition
two or more things working together

Silverback gorillas are the leaders of their troops. They decide where the troop goes and what they do all day.

Silverbacks make sure *(shur)* that all the other gorillas are behaving *(bee-HAY-ving)* themselves. If a gorilla is misbehaving, the silverback can just look at them to make them stop. Other times, the silverback might have to get a bit more intimidating.

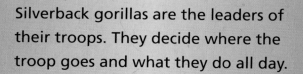

Silverbacks are also teachers. They teach younger gorillas how to fight, how to find food, and how to make nests.

Being the leader of the troop also means being the protector. Silverback gorillas are usually more aggressive than other gorillas. This is because they are in charge of the safety of their troop.

Silverbacks will try to intimidate creatures they see as a **threat** *(thret)*. They will often charge at the threat. Scientists *(SY-in-tists)* believe *(bee-LEEV)* most of these charges are just to scare threats away. However, silverback gorillas are always ready to fight if they have to.

Silverback gorillas may have to fight off other male gorillas from their troop. A younger male may want to be the new leader. If so, he will **challenge** *(CHAL-inj)* the silverback. The younger male wants to show the other gorillas that he should be the leader instead.

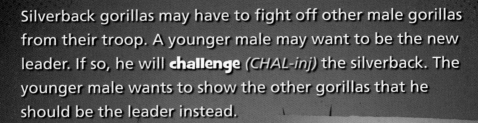

Challenge
to invite someone to take part in a contest

Sometimes, a silverback will make a challenger back down quickly. Other times, the silverback and the challenger will fight.

Silverbacks protect their troops from other gorillas. Sometimes, when two troops of gorillas meet, the two dominant silverbacks might get into a fight.

Fights between gorillas can be very violent. Scientists following *(FOL-loh-ing)* gorillas have seen deep cuts caused by their sharp fangs. Gorillas have even been known to break each other's bones in fights.

A silverback is likely to have lots of scars on their body. They come from many years of protecting their troop. Silverbacks are tough *(tuf)* fighters!

FIGHTING STYLES
(STY-ulz)

Lions hide from their prey before they attack. Hunting when the sun is down helps to keep them hidden in the savannah. While they usually hunt in packs, lions have been known to go after prey by themselves.

Lions attack from behind. It is usually safer for them to do this. It means that their prey cannot see them coming. It also keeps the lion safe if their prey has horns on its head or sharp teeth.

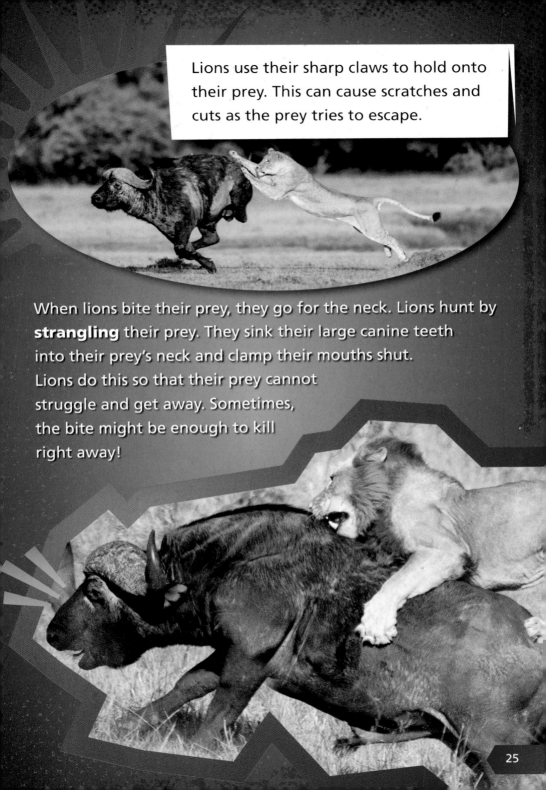

Lions use their sharp claws to hold onto their prey. This can cause scratches and cuts as the prey tries to escape.

When lions bite their prey, they go for the neck. Lions hunt by **strangling** their prey. They sink their large canine teeth into their prey's neck and clamp their mouths shut. Lions do this so that their prey cannot struggle and get away. Sometimes, the bite might be enough to kill right away!

Gorillas are usually (YOO-zhoo-uh-lee) peaceful creatures. They are not hunters that chase after prey. They only get into fights when they are **provoked**. However, once the fight starts, gorillas are very deadly.

Provoked
made someone annoyed or angry

The gorilla's sharp fangs may be the first thing it attacks with. After showing them off, the gorilla may look to sink those fangs into their **opponent** (uh-PO-nent).

Opponent
someone on the opposite (OP-puh-sit) side of a contest

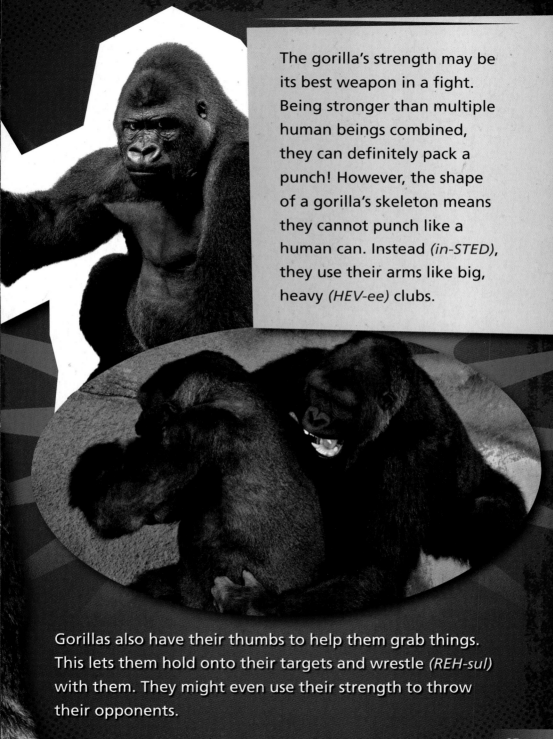

The gorilla's strength may be its best weapon in a fight. Being stronger than multiple human beings combined, they can definitely pack a punch! However, the shape of a gorilla's skeleton means they cannot punch like a human can. Instead *(in-STED)*, they use their arms like big, heavy *(HEV-ee)* clubs.

Gorillas also have their thumbs to help them grab things. This lets them hold onto their targets and wrestle *(REH-sul)* with them. They might even use their strength to throw their opponents.

TALE OF THE TAPE

After looking at our competitors, they both have a lot to offer when it comes to a fight. Let's bring it all together to look over their strengths and weaknesses.

LION

Strengths
- Sharp claws
- Skilled hunters
- Big teeth that help them catch prey
- Powerful muscles for quick movements

Weaknesses
- Not as good at hunting by themselves
- Fight in short bursts

GORILLA

Strengths
- Incredibly strong
- Thumbs that help them grab and throw things
- Sharp fangs
- Very **intelligent** (in-TEL-ih-jent)

Intelligent
clever or smart

Weaknesses
- Cannot move very fast
- Not natural (NACH-ur-ul) hunters

Of course (kors), looking at strengths and weaknesses only gives us an idea of what our competitors can do. There is only one way to find out who the best fighter really is. It is time to clash!

THE MAIN EVENT

Finally *(FY-nuh-lee)*, it is time for our main event! We will find out who will win in a fight between a lion and a gorilla.

A lion roars when it feels like a fight is coming. The dominant male lion roars to mark its territory. It lets other creatures know not to come too close, or there could be deadly **consequences** *(KON-sih-kwen-siz)*. A lion's roar can be heard from five miles away.

Consequences
the result of doing something

A gorilla also makes a big display when a fight might be about to start. Gorillas stand up on their legs and beat their chests with their hands. They also make loud hooting sounds and show off their sharp fangs.

All of this is done to try to stop another animal from attacking. However, if an animal challenges a gorilla to a fight, then a gorilla is not likely to back down. . . .

The African lion's roar rumbles across the land. The silverback gorilla hears the roar and stands up tall. It beats its chest and shouts back at the lion, warning it to not get too close. However, it cannot see the lion. The silverback is not sure where it is.

The lion sneaks up on the gorilla. It hides in the shadows (SHAD-ohz), making as little noise as possible. The silverback is in its sights.

The lion pounces toward (tword) the gorilla. The silverback only has a split-second to **react** (ree-AKT). The lion's claws dig into the gorilla's back. However, the silverback gorilla is not like the animals the lion usually hunts on the savannah.

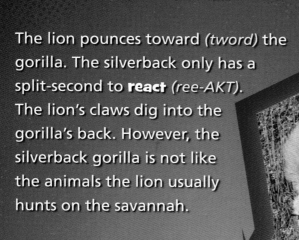

React
to act because of
something happening

The silverback is not about to go down without a fight. The gorilla struggles against the lion's sharp grip, trying to get the big cat off its back.

The gorilla uses its greatest weapons. First, it manages *(MAN-uh-jiz)* to grab a hold of the lion's mane. Then, the gorilla uses its incredible strength to throw the lion off its back. The gorilla is quick to strike. The silverback is all over the lion, wrestling with it and clubbing it with heavy blows.

Now, the lion has to fight its target face-to-face. It slashes and swipes at the silverback with its claws. The silverback is in a lot of pain.

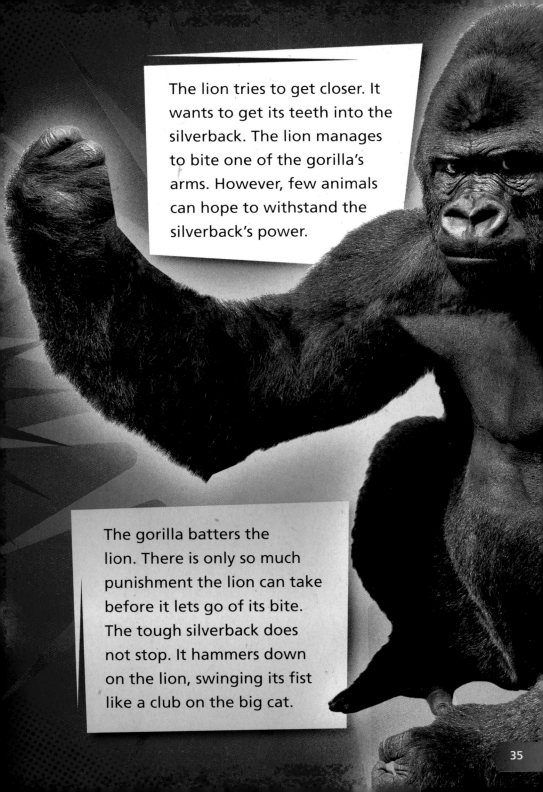

The lion tries to get closer. It wants to get its teeth into the silverback. The lion manages to bite one of the gorilla's arms. However, few animals can hope to withstand the silverback's power.

The gorilla batters the lion. There is only so much punishment the lion can take before it lets go of its bite. The tough silverback does not stop. It hammers down on the lion, swinging its fist like a club on the big cat.

The silverback gorilla's raw power proves *(proovz)* to be too much for the lion. The lion is taking a beating from the great ape. It fights back as best as it can. The lion gets in a few more scratches, but it is not enough to stop the silverback.

The lion **surrenders** *(sur-REN-durz)* and backs away. It lets out one last roar before it turns and runs back to its pride.

Surrenders
gives up

The silverback gorilla stands tall. It watches as the lion **retreats** (ree-TREETS). The silverback beats its chest in victory (VIK-tur-ree). It howls and **hollers**, letting anyone that can hear know that it is the winner.

Retreats
backs away from a battle during or after a loss

Although it has won, the silverback will not forget this battle. The lion's teeth and claws will leave plenty of scars. It was a tough fight that could have gone either way.

WINNER:
THE SILVERBACK GORILLA

ACTION REPLAY

The lion had a great start to the fight. Being able to sneak up on your opponent is always a good **advantage** *(ad-VAN-tij)* in a battle. However, the silverback gorilla is very different from all of the animals that lions hunt in the savannah.

Advantage
something that puts you in a better spot to do something

The lion was not able to bite into the gorilla's neck. If it had, then the fight may have played out very differently.

Once *(wuns)* the gorilla grabbed a hold of the lion, it was hard for the lion to fight back. The lion was not used *(yoost)* to standing on its back legs for such a long time. The gorilla was much better at fighting standing up.

The lion tends to use its power in short bursts. It was not able to keep up with the gorilla as the fight went on. The gorilla's toughness and power wore the lion down.

REMATCH?

Do you think the right animal won this fight?

Gorillas and lions come from different habitats. It is unlikely that they would ever come to blows in real life.

In any fight, there are always things that could have gone differently. What if they were deep in the jungle? Or on the savannah plains? What if it was a pack of lionesses on the hunt? What if the silverback had support from the rest of its troop?

This was just one battle. The animal kingdom has all kinds of fighters waiting for a chance to be in the spotlight.

Which animals would you like to see get into the combat zone? Would any other animal dare to challenge a silverback gorilla? Who will rise up and become our next **champion** (CHAM-pee-un)?

Champion
the winner of
a contest

GLOSSARY

common *(KOM-mun)*
a detail that is shared between two things

competitor *(kum-PEH-tih-tur)*
someone taking part in a contest

force *(fors)*
the strength of an action or movement

hollers
makes a loud noise

primate *(PRY-mate)*
the group of animals that contain humans, apes, and monkeys

savannah *(suh-VAN-nuh)*
large areas of flat ground with grass and trees that are found in hot places

strangling
squeezing that can stop breathing

threat *(thret)*
something that is likely to cause harm